Volcanoes
of the National Parks in Hawai'i

D0403798

Gordon A. Macdonald
Former Director, Hawaiian Volcano Observatory, U.S. Geological Survey

Douglass H. Hubbard
Former Chief Park Naturalist, Hawai'i Volcanoes National Park

2007 Update by Christina Heliker and Donald Swanson
Hawaiian Volcano Observatory, U.S. Geological Survey

HAWAI'I NATURAL HISTORY ASSOCIATION

Twelfth Edition, 2007
© 2007 Hawai'i Natural History Association
Hawai'i National Park, Hawai'i 96718
http://www.hawaiinaturalhistory.org/

Published in cooperation with the National Park Service

 This publication printed entirely on recycled paper.

ISBN 978-0-940295-01-8

Introduction

Three active volcanoes became Hawai'i National Park by an act of Congress on August 1, 1916. The new park included parts of Kīlauea and Mauna Loa on the island of Hawai'i, and Haleakalā on Maui. In 1961 the park was divided into Hawai'i Volcanoes National Park and Haleakalā National Park.

Both parks protect the natural beauty and unique ecosystems of their volcanic mountains. Kīlauea and Mauna Loa are two of the largest and most active volcanoes on earth. Dormant Haleakalā, with its stark, otherworldly landscape,

With native ferns and trees providing a backdrop (left), the fortunate few who visit Kīlauea when it is in eruption witness an awesome and beautiful spectacle.

is one of the world's most colorful volcanic sights.

In many volcanic regions, people flee in terror from an eruption, accustomed as they are to violent explosions that claim many lives. In Hawai'i, however, spectators rush to the scene of an eruption, knowing that much of the activity can be safely viewed at close range. Other volcanoes on earth may be just as docile, but few are as accessible. Many eruptions of Kīlauea, in particular, can be approached without difficulty.

Each year millions of people visit Hawai'i Volcanoes and Haleakalā to view the results of past volcanic activity. The fortunate few who visit Kīlauea or Mauna Loa when they are erupting gaze in awe at great lava fountains, seething lakes of molten rock, or incandescent rivers of flowing lava. It is the intent of this book to provide a brief explanation of volcanic activity in Hawai'i and the resulting land forms, in the belief that a better understanding of what one sees will enhance the pleasure of seeing it.

Geologic Setting

Nowhere on earth can you be more distant from a large continent than on the chain of islands and seamounts, stretching for more than 1,500 miles, that forms the Hawaiian Archipelago. Mere specks of land in the vast Pacific Ocean, the Hawaiian Islands are the tops of a great volcanic mountain range built up from the sea floor by thousands upon thousands of volcanic eruptions. The average depth of the ocean around the island chain is over 15,000 feet, so even the lowest islands are towering mountains. On the island of Hawai'i, Mauna Kea and Mauna Loa rise more than 30,000 feet above their base on the sea floor. Mauna Kea is the highest peak in the Pacific Ocean, and Mauna Loa is the world's tallest mountain as measured from its base on the sea floor.

The origin of the Hawaiian islands has long been of interest to scientists. The first geologists to study the problem hypothesized that the volcanoes formed simultaneously over a great fissure on the sea floor and that the volcanoes to the northwest went extinct more quickly. With the advent of plate tectonic theory in the early 1960s, the age progression of the islands received a new explanation. The earth's lithosphere, the solid outer layer composed of the crust and upper mantle, is divided into many rigid plates that drift upon the more fluid asthenosphere. Plate margins, where adjacent plates collide, spread apart, or slide past one another, are zones of enormous geologic change.

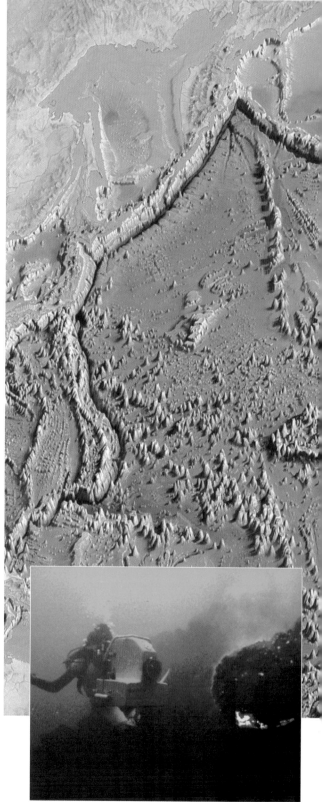

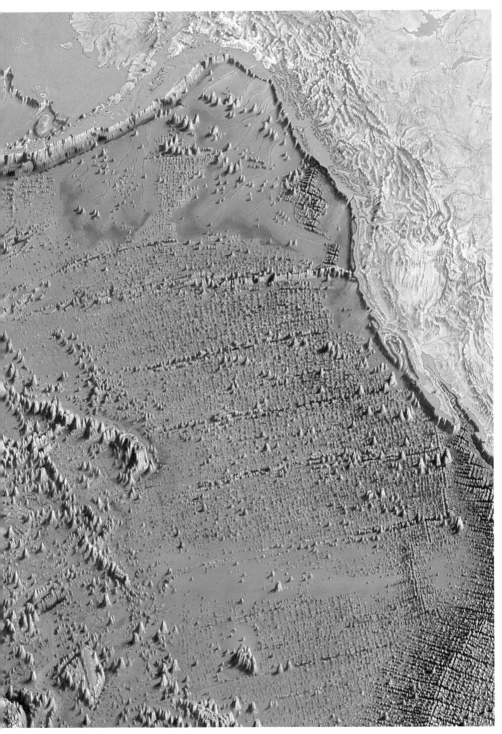

Located in the northern Pacific Ocean, the Hawaiian Archipelago is the most isolated island chain in the world. Recent volcanic activity has given researchers a chance to study the interaction between lava and the ocean water typical of the island-building process (left).

Most of the world's earthquakes and volcanic activity takes place at plate margins. Hawai'i, however, sits in the middle of the Pacific Plate. The source of magma that fuels Hawaiian volcanoes is a "hot spot" in the earth's mantle. The hot spot heats rock, which melts, rises, and eventually erupts. As the Pacific Plate drifts to the northwest over the hot spot, islands are born. Each volcano eventu-

Many of the Earth's volcanic regions are found along the edges of moving tectonic plates, while Hawai'i is located over a volcanic hot spot in the middle of the Pacific Plate. As the plate drifts in a northwesterly direction (below), the islands are slowly carried away from the hot spot. The older volcanoes, cut off from their source of magma, become dormant and then extinct as new islands begin to form at the southern end of the chain (right).

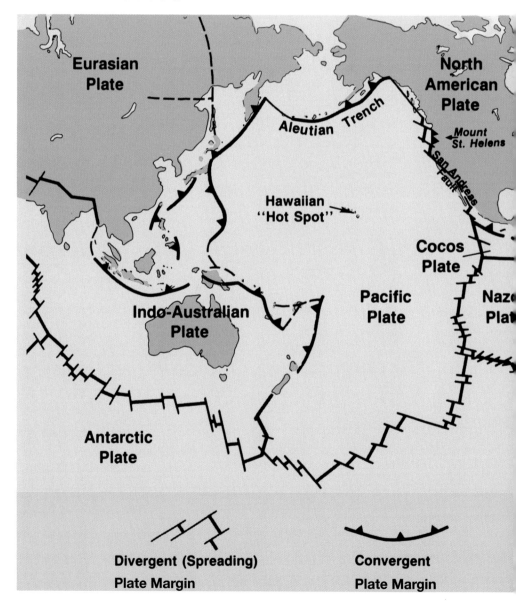

Eurasian Plate

North American Plate

Aleutian Trench

Mount St. Helens

San Andreas Fault

Hawaiian "Hot Spot"

Cocos Plate

Indo-Australian Plate

Pacific Plate

Nazca Plate

Antarctic Plate

Divergent (Spreading) Plate Margin

Convergent Plate Margin

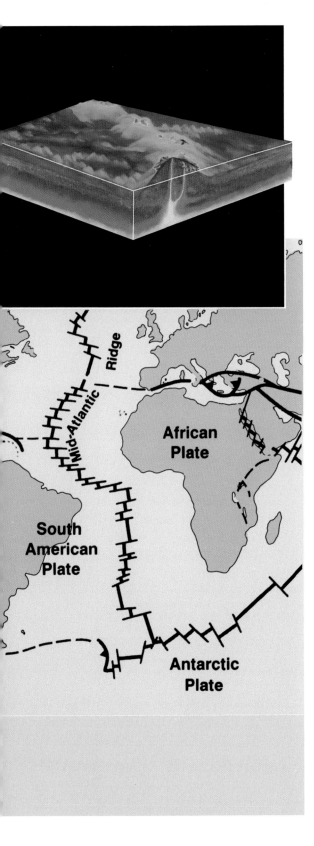

ally is carried away from the hot spot and becomes extinct. Thus, each of the Hawaiian islands began in the same general location as the present island of Hawai'i.

The long chain of islands and seamounts, 70 million years old, is testimony to the steady northwestward drift of the Pacific Plate. The current rate of movement is about two inches a year. The oldest rocks of Kaua'i, the northwesternmost of the main islands, are five to seven million years old. By contrast, the oldest rocks on the island of Hawai'i erupted less than one million years ago.

Even as a young Hawaiian volcano is still growing upward from the ocean floor, the erosive force of waves and landslides begins to reduce its edifice. When the volcano rises above sea level, new destructive forces come into play. Waves, wind, rain, streams, and, rarely, even glaciers carve the new island and carry sediment back to sea. The islands slowly subside, too, because the great weight of the volcanoes bows down the crust beneath the islands. As long as the volcano is active, however, the island will continue to grow. But as the island is slowly rafted away from the hot spot and its eruptions become less frequent and then stop, the island gradually wastes away. Deep valleys are carved by streams, and coral reefs encircle the coastline.

In addition to the gradual processes of erosion and subsidence, catastrophic loss of the entire flank of a volcano due to gigantic landslides is also part of the life history of many Hawaiian volcanoes. The deposits from these landslides have been discovered in the last 20 years by extensive undersea mapping around the Hawaiian Islands. Large parts of the north sides of Koʻolau Volcano (Oʻahu) and of East Molokaʻi Volcano were swept away by massive landslides. These landslides occur every few tens of thousands of years, so the probability of one happening in our lifetime is very small.

As the Pacific plate creeps northwestward, the older islands are worn away until the evidence of their volcanic origin is hidden by coral reefs and atolls. The visible parts of Kure and Midway Islands are formed entirely of limestone and calcareous sand—the remains of calcite-secreting coral and algae. But at a depth of only a few hundred feet, the limestone sits on the truncated summits of great volcanic mountains.

After tens of thousands of years of erosion, some volcanoes enter a period of renewed activity, know as the "rejuvenation stage." The islands of Kauaʻi and Oʻahu were deeply eroded before rejuvenation-stage eruptions buried much of the lowlands.

Hawaiʻi, the southeasternmost of the islands and the youngest, is built of five volcanoes. Kohala, at the northwest end of the island, is the oldest, and landslides and erosion have transformed its rainy northeast slope into spectacular canyons. Mauna Kea, which last erupted about 4,500 years ago, holds the distinction of being the only Hawaiian volcano known to have had a summit glacier during the last ice age. The terminal moraines of this glacier are still readily visible above the Mauna Kea State Recreation Area in the saddle between Mauna Loa and Mauna Kea. Hualālai, which rises above Kailua-Kona, last erupted in 1801. The two southernmost volcanoes, Mauna Loa and Kīlauea, have both erupted numerous times in the last two centuries.

The larger islands in the chain receive abundant rainfall, and even the active volcanoes are cloaked in verdant tropical vegetation. The remnants of ancient volcanoes that make up the islands to the northwest, however, are too small to collect moisture from the prevailing trade winds. Although waterless, these atolls are home to the endangered Hawaiian monk seal and provide nesting sites for countless seabirds. The Hawaiian Islands National Wildlife Refuge was established in 1909 to protect the northwestern islands and their creatures.

Nāpali Coast on the island of Kauaʻi (top) shows the effect of millions of years of erosion and landslides, with steep cliffs cut into the side of volcanic ridges. The islands are actually the tops of volcanic peaks, which rise from the ocean floor (bottom). Ocean depths and land elevations are indicated by color, from purple in the Hawaiian moat (19,700 ft deep) to white on top of Mauna Loa and Mauna Kea (13,796 ft high). Historical lava flows on the Island of Hawaiʻi are shown in red.

Wai'anae   Ko'olau

West Moloka'i   East Moloka'i

Moloka'i

Lāna'i

Lāna'i   West Maui

Maui

Kaho'olawe   Haleakalā

Kaho'olawe

Mahukona   Kohala

Hualalai   Mauna Kea

Hawai'i

Kilauea

Mauna Loa

Lō'ihi

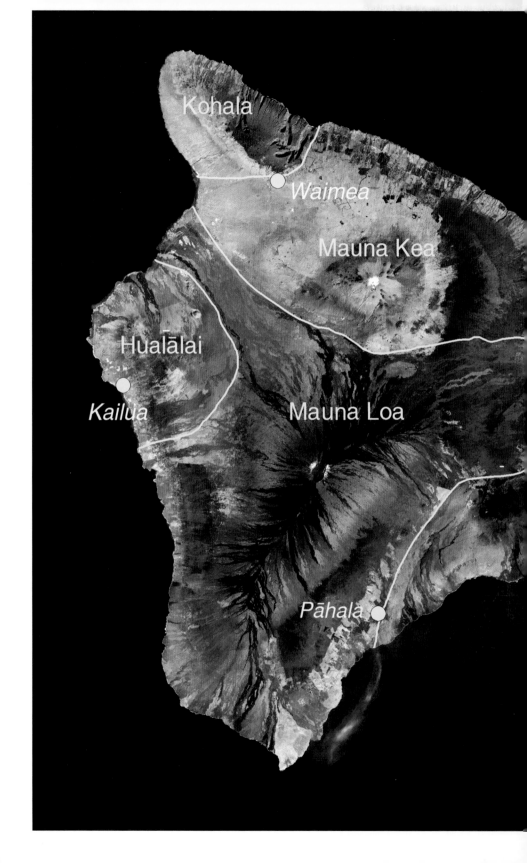

Five volcanoes, Kohala, Mauna Kea, Hualālai, Mauna Loa, and Kīlauea make up the island of Hawai'i. The two southernmost volcanoes, Mauna Loa and Kīlauea, provide a natural laboratory for the study of active volcanoes (left). Scientists study samples collected during eruptions to determine mineral and gas content (right).

Character of Hawaiian Volcanic Activity

Composition of Lava. A volcano is an opening in the earth's crust from which molten rock and gases are released. The molten rock is a complex solution of silicates, oxides, and gases called magma; when it reaches the surface of the earth, it is called lava. The gases, primarily water vapor and carbon dioxide, may be dissolved in the magma or be enclosed in it as bubbles. Magma also contains solid crystals of various minerals that form as the magma ascends to the surface.

Lava ranges widely in composition. The most abundant oxide in lava is silica (silicon dioxide), ranging from 40 to 75 percent. As the percentage of silica increases, so does that of sodium and potassium, and as it decreases the percentage of iron, magnesium, and calcium increases. Most Hawaiian lava is near the lower end of the silica scale. The most common lava extruded by Kīlauea and Mauna Loa is *olivine basalt*. Olivine, a

Average Chemical Composition of Lava

Element	Oxide Symbol	Percentage	
		Hawaiian Volcanoes	Mt. St. Helens
Silicon	SiO_2	48.4	63.5
Aluminum	Al_2O_3	13.2	17.6
Iron	FeO	11.2	4.2
Magnesium	MgO	9.7	2.0
Calcium	CaO	10.3	5.2
Sodium	Na_2O	2.4	4.6
Potassium	K_2O	0.6	1.3
Titanium	TiO_2	2.8	0.6
Other		1.4	1.0

The above table shows the difference in average chemical composition between Hawaiian lava and lava erupted by Mt. St. Helens in 1980. Numbers given represent the amount (in weight percent) of each oxide present in the lava.

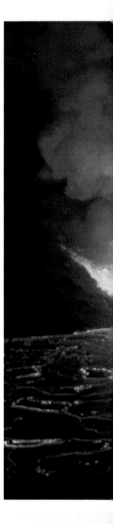

green mineral composed of iron, magnesium, and silica, commonly occurs as grains in a stony matrix of other minerals. The crystals may reach a length of half an inch but are generally smaller. Crystals of olivine are abundant at the Green Sand Beach (Papakōlea) near South Point (Kalae), where they have eroded from a nearby cone. Large black crystals of *augite* (another iron-magnesium silicate) occur in the lava and *cinder cones* of Mauna Kea and Haleakalā.

Using a pyrometer, a scientist measures the temperature of an advancing flow (above). Hawaiian names have been accepted world wide as terms for two types of lava. A pāhoehoe flow appears smooth and ropy (above, right), while an ʻaʻā flow is jumbled and clinkery (bottom, right).

Olivine basalt grades into a rock known as *andesite*, which is richer in silica than basalt and generally lighter in color. Andesite is unknown at Kīlauea and Mauna Loa but is abundant on Mauna Kea and Haleakalā; the most common variety is referred to as *hawaiite*.

Two types of lava flows occur in Hawai'i, and their Hawaiian names, *pāhoehoe* and *'a'ā,* are used by scientists around the world to describe similar lava. Pāhoehoe is characterized by a smooth, ropy, or billowy surface; it is hotter and retains more gas than 'a'ā, which has a very rough or jumbled surface but a dense interior. As a pāhoehoe flow cools and crystallizes, it may turn into an 'a'ā flow, and fluid lava inside an 'a'ā flow may spill out to form pāhoehoe. The difference between the two types has nothing to do with chemical composition but rather is a function of temperature and gas and crystal content.

'A'ā flows are fed by fast-moving rivers of lava that have been clocked at speeds as high as 35 miles per hour on steep slopes. From the river channel, lava spreads laterally to feed the moving flow margins, but the greatest volume moves downhill to feed the flow front. The front of an 'a'ā flow travels at much slower speeds than the feeding channel. These flows can suddenly surge forward, however, as lava that has ponded behind the flow front reaches a critical thickness and overcomes the barrier of cooler lava that has held it back. When 'a'ā flows devastated the Royal Gardens subdivision in 1983-85, geologists observed flows that surged several hundred feet in just a few minutes.

When an eruption ends, the fluid lava may drain away, leaving a distinct channel lower than the surrounding flow. Such a channel can be seen along the Chain of Craters Road at Muliwai a Pele, in a 1973 flow from Mauna Ulu.

Pāhoehoe flows can form fast-moving channels or slow-moving crusted flows fed by lava tubes. Lava tubes develop in channeled flows as crust accumulates on the margins of the channel, eventually forming a roof across the flowing lava. Tubes insulate the lava stream and allow it to travel much farther before cooling and stagnating. From late 1986 through 2006, lava tubes frequently extended from vents on the middle east rift zone of Kīlauea to the ocean eight miles away. When activity at a vent ceases, most of the lava in a tube may drain away, leaving a tunnel with an arched ceiling and flat floor. Lava tubes may have "high lava" marks from changes in the level of the lava stream in the tube.

Nature of Hawaiian Eruptions. Most of the world's volcanoes erupt violently. Why, then, are most Hawaiian eruptions relatively benign? The reason is that Hawaiian magma is more fluid than magma at more explosive volcanoes and has a lower gas content, about 0.5 to 0.7 percent by weight. The viscosity of any lava is governed by three primary factors: its temperature, its chemical composition, and the amount of gas it contains. The lower the silica content of the lava, the less viscous it is; also, the higher the temperature and gas content, the lower the viscosity.

When lava is very viscous, the enclosed gas builds up to a high pressure before escaping with explosive violence. When this happens near populated areas, the result can be devastating, as it was during the 1980 eruption of Mount St. Helens and the 1991 eruption of Pinatubo in the Philippines. In contrast, Hawaiian olivine basalt is low in silica, releases gases easily, and is extremely hot (generally 1,100-1,180°C, or 2,012-2,156°F), resulting in fluid lava. Episodes of high fountaining, during which lava can soar over a thousand feet into the air, are as vigorous as most Hawaiian eruptions get.

Pāhoehoe flows cool more quickly along their outer edges, often forming a channel that restricts the flow. A lava tube results when the cooling edges begin to form a roof over the flow (right), enclosing and insulating the molten stream. Lava may travel great distances within tubes before breaking out and again reaching the surface (left). When activity ceases, lava may drain from the tube, leaving a cave-like formation (inset).

Although violent explosions accompany only a small percent of all Hawaiian eruptions, Kīlauea does erupt explosively every few hundred years, or about as often as does Mount St. Helens. And, of all the volcanoes now in the United States, Kīlauea has been the most lethal, with an explosive eruption in AD 1790 killing between about 80 and 800 people. Explosive eruptions in Hawai'i, however, are small compared with such cataclysms as the eruption of Krakatau in Indonesia in 1883 or of Alaska's Katmai in 1912. Some explosive eruptions in Hawai'i are caused by the interaction of magma with either ground water or surface water.

The fluid nature of Hawaiian lava is demonstrated by the formation of tree molds and lava trees. When pāhoehoe surrounds a tree, the lava chills against the tree trunk and hardens, preserving many of the details of the bark. After the tree has burned, a cylindrical hole, or tree mold, remains where the tree once stood. Frequently the surface of the flow subsides as lava drains away, leaving the lava that solidified around a trunk as a lava tree that can be more than 10 feet tall.

The composition of Hawaiian lava allows it to release gas easily, resulting in eruptions characterized by fountains of various heights and lava lake activity (left). In contrast, a high build-up of gases precipitated the devastating 1980 eruption of Mount St. Helens (inset).

Surface Deformation of Hawaiian Volcanoes. Early in the history of the Hawaiian Volcano Observatory, scientists determined that the slopes of Kīlauea and Mauna Loa were constantly deforming, and that this movement correlated with activity of the volcano. Prior to an eruption the volcano swells or inflates, causing its flanks to tilt outwards. Following the eruption the volcano contracts or deflates, and the slopes tilt inward. These changes can be measured by leveling, a technique used in land surveys. By leveling from sea level at Hilo, scientists found that from 1912 to 1921 a benchmark near the

Some eruptions involve a line of fountains issuing from a fissure, while others will have only a single vent (right). As flows from such eruptions move through forested areas, lava trees may be formed (above), sculpted around the trunks of native 'ōhi'a (left) or other trees.

observatory had risen nearly three feet. After the great collapse and explosions of 1924, the same benchmark had subsided 3.5 feet, while a benchmark near the rim of Halemaʻumaʻu dropped about 13 feet.

Tilting of the ground surface is now usually measured by electronic instruments called tiltmeters. An increase in outward tilt, when accompanied by swarms of earthquakes, is an indication that magma is rising in the volcano and that an eruption may be impending.

The surface of an active volcano moves sideways as well as up and down. A swelling magma body or an intruding dike causes horizontal deformation at the surface. This movement is measured by electronic surveying and satellite-based Global Positioning System (GPS) methods.

Ground deformation and earthquake patterns indicate that Kīlauea has a shallow magma storage reservoir at a depth of 0.5 to 2.5 miles below the summit, whereas the source of magma lies at least 30 to 40 miles below the surface. Similarly, Mauna Loa has a shallow reservoir about 2.5 miles beneath its summit.

Mauna Loa: World's Largest Mountain and Still Growing

Description. Of all the world's active volcanoes, none approaches the immensity of Mauna Loa (long mountain), the largest single mountain mass on earth. From its base on the down-bowed sea floor, Mauna Loa rises 56,000 feet, of which 13,677 feet are above sea level. Mauna Loa has a volume of over 18,000 cubic miles, compared with 80 cubic miles for California's Mount Shasta, the largest volcano in the Cascade Range. Mauna Loa's bulk has been built almost entirely by the accumulation of thousands of thin lava flows, averaging only 10 to 15 feet in thickness.

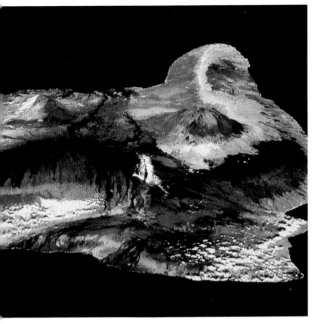

Mauna Loa is a dome-shaped shield volcano with very broad, gentle slopes no steeper than 12 degrees; similar slopes extend to the sea floor. At the volcano's summit is an oval-shaped depression three miles long, one-and-a-half miles wide, and up to 600 feet deep. This depression, or caldera, which formed by collapse of the summit, is named Moku'āweoweo. At the northern and southern ends of the caldera, Moku'āweoweo merges with

The broad basaltic shields of Mauna Loa and Kīlauea are visible in this satellite image (top). Layer upon layer of lava flows have given Mauna Loa its distinctive dome shape, with gently sloping flanks (left). A closer look, however, would reveal the cones and spatter ramparts that attest to recent activity at these shield volcanoes (above, right).

smaller, nearly circular pit craters also formed by collapse.

Two prominent zones of fracturing called rift zones extend from Mauna Loa's summit caldera. These zones of weakness are marked at the surface by open fissures and by cinder and spatter cones built up during eruptions by the accumulation of fragments of lava ejected into the air. Loosely cemented cinder cones are composed of bits of lava that cool and solidify before falling back to earth. Spatter cones are welded together from blobs of

lava that are still partly molten when they hit the ground.

Mauna Loa's southwest rift zone extends from the summit to the coast west of Kalae (South Point). The northeast rift zone extends from Moku'āweoweo toward Hilo. When Mauna Loa is viewed from the Thomas A. Jaggar Museum, on the rim of Kīlauea, the northeast rift zone is marked by a succession of cinder cones, the most prominent being Pu'u'ula'ula (Red Hill), at 10,000 feet.

The slopes of Mauna Loa show many variations in color, depending on the age and surface characteristics of the lava flows.

Fresh 'a'ā flows from the rift zones appear black, and fresh pāhoehoe flows may appear shiny silver-gray in the sunlight. Older flows are dark gray, and still older ones, reddish-brown. Actively moving lava flows frequently branch, surrounding older areas and leaving small "islands" of undisturbed land called kīpuka in Hawai'i. On the upper slopes of the mountain, the newer black flows surround kīpuka of older lava. On the lower slopes the kīpuka are islands of vegetation, many with large old trees. Kīpukakī and Kīpukapuaulu on the Mauna Loa Strip Road are good examples.

Before Kīlauea formed, the southeast flank of Mauna Loa was subject to giant landslides. Deep canyons in the Nīnole Hills, prominent flat-topped features above the highway between Pāhala and Nā'ālehu, were cut after massive landslide failure of the old south flank of Mauna Loa.

Mauna Loa Generates both Earthquakes and Eruptions. Earthquakes beneath active Hawaiian volcanoes generally are related to stresses in the earth's crust induced by the movement of magma. On November 16, 1983, a magnitude 6.6 earthquake took place in the Ka'ōiki fault system beneath the southeast flank of Mauna Loa, just outside Hawai'i Volcanoes National Park. In less than one minute, more than $8 million of damage was incurred—fortunately without loss of life. Four months later, Mauna Loa erupted.

The largest Hawaiian earthquake in recorded history was in 1868 and had an estimated magnitude of between 7.5 and 8.1. This earthquake also originated

beneath the southeast flank of Mauna Loa, in the general vicinity of Wood Valley. The 1868 earthquake caused damage across the entire island and was felt as far away as the island of Kaua'i. The devastation was greatest in the

Sections of Crater Rim Drive in Hawai'i Volcanoes National Park were permanently closed to traffic after severe earthquake damage in 1983 (top). Except for a small eruption in 1975 (upper right), Mauna Loa was quiet between 1950 and 1984, and its summit caldera was often blanketed with snow (right).

Ka'ū district, where the earthquake triggered both a mudflow and a local tsunami, killing at least 79 people.

Throughout the last two centuries, Mauna Loa has erupted more than 5.7 billion cubic yards of lava. During this time, eruptions have broken out at or near the summit caldera, then migrated to

vents along one of the rift zones or to isolated vents on the northwest flank.

Typically, an eruption begins with the opening of one or more fissures that may extend as far as 13 miles. A nearly continuous line of lava fountains, from a few feet to several hundred feet high, play from the fissures. The voluminous outpouring of lava soon forms fast-moving flows, and spatter ramparts build up along the fissure system. The row of fountains is short-lived, usually lasting less than a day. Much of the fissure then becomes inactive, and the eruption is localized at a few individual vents. Fountains may then increase in height, reaching as high as 800 feet. Debris from the fountains accumulates around the vent, forming a cinder or spatter cone. Pumice and Pele's hair (natural spun glass) formed during high fountaining drift downwind for great distances. During this stage of eruption, massive lava flows issue from the vents and can continue to flow for days to months. Many flows erupted from Mauna Loa in the last two centuries have reached the sea, adding new land to the island.

The Most Recent Eruption of Mauna Loa. At 1:25 A.M., on March 25, 1984, lava began fountaining from fissures on the floor of Mokuʻāweoweo. Shortly thereafter, eruptive fissures opened on the southwest rift zone, and within a few hours the eruption had spread to the northeast rift zone. By 7:00 A.M., lava was erupting only at the 12,500-foot level on the northeast rift zone. Seismometers indicated that magma was moving downrift toward Puʻuʻulaʻula, at 10,000 feet. Hikers along the trail to the summit were advised of the danger and escorted off the mountain.

Hawaiian Volcano Observatory scientists monitored the downrift migration of earthquakes and

Mauna Kea rises in the background as lava fountains play during the brief summit eruption of Mauna Loa in 1975 (above). This outbreak set the stage for flank activity in 1984, when a series of fissures opened up along the volcano's northeast rift zone (right and upper right), eventually feeding rivers of lava that crisscrossed for miles down Mauna Loa's slopes during the three-week-long eruption (left).

watched for surface activity near the leading edge of the earthquake swarm. At 9:00 A.M. a helicopter landed near the anticipated outbreak, which began within minutes. By mid-morning, a nearly mile-long fissure opened and erupted nearly two million cubic yards of lava an hour, feeding 200-foot high fountains and a lava flow that advanced to the southeast. This activity continued until late afternoon, when fissures ruptured the ground at the 9,400-foot level and upslope activity came to an end.

Lava continued to flow from these latest vents for the next 21 days, briefly threatening the city of Hilo but ultimately stagnating five miles away. Mauna Loa's 1984 eruption was the largest since 1950 but extruded only about 60 percent as much lava. Much of the lava erupted in 1984 apparently intruded the northeast rift zone during a 19-hour summit eruption in 1975.

Following the 1984 eruption of Mauna Loa, a V-shaped diversionary wall was constructed above the Mauna Loa Observatory, NOAA's climate monitoring station on the northern slope of the volcano, in hopes of protecting the facility during future eruptions. Other areas will be harder to protect. As development on the island accelerates, local government must bear in mind the potentially devastating effects a prolonged major eruption of Mauna Loa could have on the island's residents and its economy.

Seen from the summit of Kīlauea, a glow which lit the sky and could be seen from miles away confirmed the start of the March 1984 eruption of Mauna Loa (left). Scientists flew over the eruption site as soon as possible, and by morning were in the field to take measurements and samples and to study the characteristics of the most recent rift eruption (above). Down slope, pockets of lush vegetation may be found in areas unaffected by activity for hundreds of years (far left).

Eruptions of Mauna Loa[1]

Year	Month and day	Summit eruption	Flank eruption	Location of principal outflow	Altitude main vent	Approximate repose period since last eruption (months)	Area of lava flow (sq. miles)	Volume (cu. yards in millions)
		Approximate duration (days)						
1832	June 20	21	(?)	Summit	13,000 (?)	—	—	—
1843	Jan. 10	5	90	N. flank	9,800	126	17.4	265
1849	May 5 (?)	15	—	Summit	[2]13,000	73	0.8	33
1851	Aug. 8	4	—	Summit	13,300	26	4.6	46
1852	Feb. 17	1	20	N.E. rift	8,400	6	12.7	238
1855	Aug. 11	<1	450	N.E. rift	10,500(?)	41	[3]25.5	367
1859	Jan. 23	<1	300	N. flank	9,200	26	[4]35.1	[4]502
1865	Dec. 30	125	—	Summit	13,000	732	1.9	66
1868	Mar. 27	<1	[5]5	S. rift	3,300	23	[4]9.3	[4]161
1871	Aug. 10	20	—	Summit	13,000	18	1.2	26
1872	Aug. 9	[6]1200	—	Summit	13,300	11	[6]1.9	[6]825
1877	Feb. 14	<1	[7]<1	W. flank	-180+	12	0.4	10
1879	Mar. 9	<1	—	Summit	13,000	12	0.4	1
1880	May 1	6	—	Summit	13,000	38	1.9	13
1880	Nov. 5	—	280	N.E. rift	10,400	6	19.7	170
1887	Jan. 16	<1	7	S.W. rift	5,700	65	[4]11.2	[4]168
1892	Nov. 30	3	—	Summit	13,000	68	1.2	16
1896	Apr. 21	16	—	Summit	13,000	41	1.9	33
1899	July 1	4	21	N.E. rift	10,700	38	8.9	106
1903	Sept. 1	<1	—	Summit	13,000	46	0.4	4
1903	Oct. 6	61	—	Summit	13,000	50	1.9	92
1907	Jan. 9	<1	15	S.W. rift	6,200	37	10.8	159
1914	Nov. 25	48	—	Summit	13,000	94	1.9	72
1916	May 19	—	12	S.W. rift	7,400	16	6.6	41
1919	Sept. 26	<1	38	S.W. rift	7,700	40	[4]10.8	[4]240
1926	Apr. 10	<1	14	S.W. rift	7,600	77	13.5	[4]159
1933	Dec. 2	17	—	Summit	13,000	91	2.3	131
1935	Nov. 21	6	40	N.E. rift	12,100	23	[8]12.7	114
1940	Apr. 17	134	—	Summit	13,000	51	[9]5.0	144
1942	Apr. 26	2	13	N.E. rift	9,200	20	[10]13.1	231
1949	Jan. 6	145	—	Summit	13,000	61	8.5	152
1950	June 1	1	23	S.W. rift	8,000	12	43.2	493
1975	July 5	1	—	Summit	13,000	301	5.0	[11]39
1984	Mar. 26	<1	22	N.E. rift	9,500	106	18.5	[11]288

[1] The duration for most of the eruptions previous to 1899 is only approximate. Heavy columns of fume at Mokuʻāweoweo, apparently representing copious gas release accompanied by little or no lava discharge, were observed in January 1870, December 1887, March 1921, November 1943, and August 1944. They are indicated in the table.

[2] All eruptions in the caldera are listed at 13,000 feet altitude, although many of them were a little lower.

[3] Upper end of the flow cannot be identified with certainty.

[4] Area above sea level. The volume below sea level is unknown, but estimates give the following orders of magnitude: 1859 – 121,000,000 cubic yards; 1868 – 64,000,000 cubic yards; 1877 – 13,000,000 cubic yards; 1919 – 127,000,000 cubic yards; 1926 – 6,400,000 cubic yards. These are included in the volumes given in the table.

[5] Flank eruption started April 7.

[6] Activity in the summit caldera was essentially continuous from August 1872 to February 1877, only the most violent activity being visible from Hilo. Activity was noted in January and April of 1873, January and August of 1875, and February of 1876.

[7] Submarine eruption off Kealakekua, on the west coast of Hawaiʻi

[8] About 0.5 square mile of this is covered by the thin flank flow above the main cone and 0.8 square mile is in Mokuʻāweoweo caldera.

[9] 2.7 square miles is in Mokuʻāweoweo caldera and 2.4 square miles outside the caldera.

[10] 2.8 square miles of this is covered by the thin flank flow near the summit, and 0.4 square mile is in the caldera.

[11] Area and volume reports of Hawaiian Volcano Observatory.

Spatter ramparts quickly formed around vents on the mountain's upper slopes (right), while lava flowed toward the ocean. The glow in the evening sky above the city of Hilo was a nightly reminder of the flow's encroachment during the 1984 Mauna Loa eruption (above). The molten mass finally stagnated only a few miles from the nearest homes.

Kīlauea: Home of Pele, Goddess of Volcanoes

Description. Kīlauea is a shield volcano closely resembling Mauna Loa in structure. The mountain rises more than 20,000 feet above the ocean floor and has been formed largely by eruptions along two rift zones extending from the summit caldera. The surface of the southwest and east rift zones is distinguished by the presence of cracks, cinder and spatter cones, pit craters, and remnant fissures. Numerous large pit craters on the east rift zone are visible from Chain of Craters Road, and Crater Rim Drive passes over parallel fissures of the southwest rift zone. Farther down the southwest rift zone in the Ka'ū Desert is the Great Crack, which extends more than 10 miles. This fissure was active during the 1823 eruption of Kīlauea.

The Kīlauea summit caldera is two and a half miles long by two miles wide and is floored by nearly 2,600 acres of lava flows erupted since the late 19th century. In places, the caldera wall consists of a series of step-like fault blocks; at its highest, the caldera wall rises 400 feet above the floor. Near the southern edge of the caldera is the pit crater, Halema'uma'u, the primary vent for Kīlauea. In Hawaiian tradition, this or similar craters are known as Ka Lua o Pele (the pit of Pele), and serve as the home of Pele, goddess of volcanoes.

Pit craters are formed by vertical collapse, not by explosions. When a magma body drains away, leaving an underground void, the overlying rock is left unsupported and collapses. Lava from subsequent eruptions may pour into pit craters, or eruptive fissures may open inside the crater. Such fissures can extend across the crater floor, up the vertical walls to the rim, and continue beyond the crater. During the 1969-1974 eruption of Kīlauea at Mauna Ulu, 'Ālo'i Crater was completely filled with lava from a fissure that cut the crater wall.

Many fault scarps occur on Kīlauea. Along the rift zones elongate blocks of rock have sunk down between two parallel faults, leaving long narrow depressions known as *grabens* bounded by inward-facing fault scarps (cliffs caused by movement along faults). The Koa'e fault system connects the two rift zones south of the Kīlauea caldera. Just past the Kulanaokuaiki Campground, the Hilina Pali Road crosses the prominent Kulanaokuaiki Pali, the southernmost of the large faults in the Koa'e fault system.

On the south flank of Kīlauea are a number of fault scarps, known as the Hilina fault system, where portions of the mountain have moved downward toward the sea. Magnificent views of the Hilina fault system can be obtained from the end of the Hilina Pali Road or from Kealakomo viewpoint along Chain of Craters Road.

In the vicinity of the Kīlauea caldera, two types of volcanic debris give evidence of major explosive activity. One type is sandy ash consisting largely of basaltic glass fragments, the quickly frozen spray of lava fountains quenched by air and ground water. These deposits, gray to yellow in color, are exposed in road cuts, fault scarps, and cracks on the eastern, southern, and southwestern edges of the caldera. This material forms part of the Keanakākoʻi Ash, erupted between about 1500 and 1790. The sandy ash is much finer than the gravel-sized pumice that originated from less explosive lava fountains in the caldera and Kīlauea Iki crater. Pumice from the latter blankets the southeastern rim of the caldera, including the Devastation Trail area.

The distance between the summit caldera and an eruption on the east rift zone is illustrated by this aerial view of Kīlauea (above). The circular pit of Halemaʻumaʻu is in the lower right, and a plume of volcanic gas issues from the Puʻu ʻŌʻō vent in the distance. While eruptions add new layers of lava to the volcano (left), earthquakes also help to change the landscape, creating fault scarps when the land shifts downward and toward the sea (right).

Eruptions of Kīlauea[1]

Year	Date of Outbreak	Duration (days)	Altitude (feet)	Location	Approximate repose period since last eruption (months)[2]	Area (sq. miles)	[27]Volume (cu. yards)
1750 (?)	—	—	1,700	E. rift	—	1.57	19,500,00
1790 (?)	—	—	1,100-750	E. rift	—	3.04	37,670,00
[3]1790	Nov. (?)	—	—	Caldera	—	small lava flow	sma
1823	Feb.-July	Short	1,700-250	S.W. rift	—	[4]3.86	[4]15,000,00
1832	Jan. 14	Short	3,600	E. rim of Caldera	—	(?)	(
1840	May 30	26	3,100-750	E. rift	—	[4]6.60	[4]281,000,00
1868	April 2	Short	3,350	Kīlauea Iki	—	.07	(
1868	April 2 (?)	Short	2,550	S.W. rift	—	.04	250,00
1877	May 4	1 (?)	3,500 (?)	Caldera wall	—	(?)	(
1877	May 21 (?)	—	3,400 (?)	Keanakāko'i	—	.04	(
1884	Jan. 22[5]	1	-60 (?)	E. rift	—	(?)	(
1885	March	80 (?)	3,640 (?)	Caldera	14	(?)	(
1894	Mar. 21	6 +	3,690	Caldera	108	(?)	(
1894	July 7	4 (?)	3,690	Caldera	3.5	(?)	(
1918	Feb. 23	14	3,700	Caldera	283	.04	250,00
1919	Feb. 7	[6]294	3,700	Caldera	11	1.60	34,500,000 (
1919	Dec. 21	221	3,000	S.W. rift	1	5.00	62,000,00
1921	Mar. 18	7	3,700	Caldera	7.5	.77	8,800,00
1922	May 28	2	2,650-2,400	Makaopuhi & Nāpau	14	.04	(
1923	Aug. 25 (?)	1	3,000	E. rift (near Makaopuhi)	15	.20	100,00
[7]1924	May 10	17	—	Caldera	8	no lava flow	no lava flo
1924	July 19	11	2,365	Halema'uma'u	2.5	.02	320,00
1927	July 7	13	2,400	Halema'uma'u	35	.04	[7]3,160,00
1929	Feb. 20	2	2,500	Halema'uma'u	19	.06	1,920,00
1929	July 25	4	2,560	Halema'uma'u	5	.08	3,600,00
1930	Nov. 19	19	2,600	Halema'uma'u	15.5	.09	8,480,00
1931	Dec. 23	14	2,700	Halema'uma'u	12.5	.12	9,640,00
1934	Sept. 6	33	2,800	Halema'uma'u	44	.16	9,500,00
1952	June 27	136	2,870	Halema'uma'u	212.5	.23	64,000,00
1954	May 31	3	3,180	Halema'uma'u & Caldera	18.5	.44	8,500,00
1955	Feb. 28	88	150-1,310	E. rift	8.9	6.10	120,000,00
1959	Nov. 14	36	3,500	Kīlauea Iki	53.5	.24	51,000,00
1960	Jan. 13	36	100	E. rift	0.8	4.1	155,000,00
1961	Feb. 24	1	3,150	Halema'uma'u	12.2	.02	[8]30,00
1961	Mar. 3	22	3,150	Halema'uma'u	.02	.1	350,00
1961	July 10	7	3,150	Halema'uma'u	3.5	.4	17,300,00
1961	Sept. 22	3	2,600-1,300	[9]E. rift	2.2	.3	3,000,00
1962	Dec. 7	2	3,250-3,100	[10]E. rift	14.4	.02	430,00
1963	Aug. 21	2	3,150-2,700	[11]E. rift	8.4	.06	1,100,00
1963	Oct. 5	1	2,750-2,300	[12]E. rift	1.4	1.3	9,000,00
1965	Mar. 5	10	3,000-2,300	[13]E. rift	17.0	3.0	23,000,00
1965	Dec. 24	<1	3,150-3,000	[14]E. rift	9.5	.23	1,160,00
1967	Nov. 5	251	3,150	Halema'uma'u	23.3	.25	110,000,00
1968	Aug. 22	5	2,900-1,900	[15]E. rift	1.3	.01	[16]176,00
1968	Oct. 7	15	3,000-2,400	[17]E. rift	1.3	.8	9,000,00
1969	Feb. 22	6	3,100-2,900	[18]E. rift	4.0	2.3	22,000,00
1969	May 24	[19]867	3,150	[20]E. rift	2.0	19.3	242,000,00
1971	Aug. 14	<1	3,660-3,600	Caldera	[21]0	.8	[22]10,500,00
1971	Sept. 24	5	3,740-2,730	Caldera & S.W. rift	0	1.5	12,400,00
1972	Feb. 4	[19]455	3,150	[20]E. rift	4	13.5	163,800,00
1973	May 5	<1	3,340-3,250	[23]E. rift	0	.1	[24]1,600,00
1973	Nov. 10	30	3,250-2,900	[25]E. rift	0	.4	3,700,00
1973	Dec. 12	[19]203	3,150	[20]E. rift	1	3.1	39,300,00
1974	July 19	3	3,600-3,250	Caldera & E. rift	0	1.2	9,000,00
1974	Sept. 19	<1	3,680	Caldera	2	.4	[26]14,000,00
1974	Dec. 31	<1	3,600	S.W. rift	3	2.9	[22]19,600,00
1975	Nov. 29	1	3,600-3,520	Caldera	11	0.1	300,00
1977	Sept. 13	18	2,088-1,600	E. rift	21.5	3.0	45,000,00
1979	Nov. 16	1	3,270-3,200	E. rift	26.3	0.1	800,00
1982	Apr. 30	<1	1,080	Caldera	29.5	0.3	500,00
1982	Sept. 25	<1	1,080	Caldera	4.8	>1.0	3,000,00
[28]1983	Jan. 3	>8,346	2,180-2,380	E. rift	3.2	>45	>3,700,000,00

[1] Many eruptions have occurred on the floor of the caldera, but only a few of the later ones are listed here, data being inadequate or totally lacking for the earlier ones. On January 11, 1928, a small amount of lava was extruded on the floor of Halema'uma'u, but this is believed to have been squeezed out by the weight of a heavy landslide on the crust of the 1927 lava which was still fluid beneath (Jaggar, T.A., Volcano Letter 370, 1932).

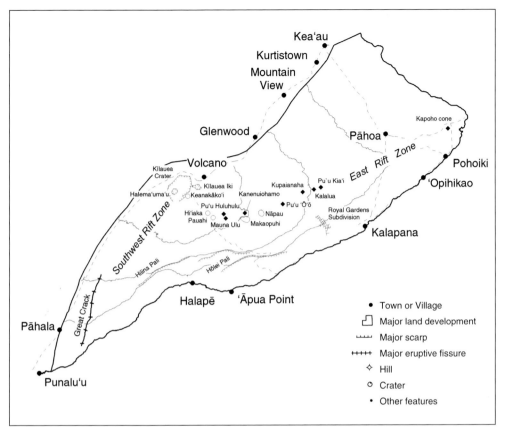

[2] During the early historic period Kīlauea caldera was observed only occasionally, and no definite record exists of the many caldera flows which are known to have occurred.

[3] Violently explosive.

[4] Area above sea level. The volume below sea level is unknown; but estimates give the following order of magnitude: 1823 — 3,000,000 cubic yards; 1840 — 200,000,000 cubic yards. These are included in the volumes given in the table.

[5] Pacific Commercial Advertiser, Feb. 2, 1884, "A column of water, like a dome, shot several hundred feet up into the air, accompanied with clouds of smoke and steam." No further eruption was observed next day.

[6] Several separate flows, with short intervals without extrusion.

[7] Violent phreatic explosions, possibly accompanied by a submarine lava flow on the E. rift.

[8] About 320,000 cubic yards of lava poured into Halemaʻumaʻu, but most of it drained back into the vents.

[9] Fourteen outbreaks along a 13-mile stretch near Nāpau Crater.

[10] Five outbreaks from ʻĀloʻi Crater to Kanenuiohamo.

[11] In and near ʻAlae Crater.

[12] In and near Nāpau Crater.

[13] Makaopuhi Crater to Kalalua Crater.

[14] In and east of ʻĀloʻi Crater.

[15] In Hiʻiaka Crater and at scattered points of 13 miles eastward.

[16] About 4,000,000 cubic yards poured into Hiʻiaka Crater, but most of it drained back into the feeding fissure at the end of the eruption.

[17] From the east flank of Kanenuiohamo for about 2 miles eastward.

[18] Between ʻAlae and Nāpau Crater.

[19] The very long duration of activity is more comparable with the long-continued activity in Halemaʻumaʻu previous to 1924 than with the other eruptions listed in this table.

[20] Mauna Ulu, between ʻAlae and Nāpau Craters.

[21] Activity was continuous at Mauna Ulu, on the E. rift.

[22] The volume is only approximate because of the difficulty in estimating the large amount that poured into open cracks.

[23] From 0.6 mile east west of Hiʻiaka Crater to Pauahi Crater.

[24] Of this, about 300,000 cubic yards drained down into fissures in the floors of the craters.

[25] From Pauahi Crater eastward 1.5 miles to near Puʻu Huluhulu.

[26] Of this, about 6,000,000 cubic yards drained down into cracks in the floor of Halemaʻumaʻu.

[27] Since 1960 all areas and volumes are based on mapping and estimates by the staff of the Hawaiian Volcano Observatory.

[28] As of this writing (November 2007) the eruption continues.

The second type of explosive debris consists of stony fragments of older lava, ranging in size from dust particles to large *blocks*, broken and thrown out by violent explosions. Several such explosions have occurred in the last few centuries: multiple explosions between about 1500 and 1790, and another in 1924. Debris from the youngest large explosion, possibly in 1790, litters the ground surface near the Hawaiian Volcano Observatory and the Thomas A. Jaggar Museum. Material from the explosions of 1924 forms the surface around Halemaʻumaʻu. One block weighing ten tons was thrown 3,500 feet east of the center of Halemaʻumaʻu on May 18, 1924.

Halemaʻumaʻu is the main vent of Kīlauea, where the volcano's principal lava conduit reaches the surface. From before 1823 until the explosive eruption of 1924, Kīlauea caldera was famous for continuously active lava lakes, mainly in Halemaʻumaʻu. During the century of lava lake activity, the upper end of the conduit contained a plug of semisolid lava. Fissures extending through this plug allowed liquid lava from below to rise to the surface, where it formed a pool about 50 feet deep. Both the plug and the fluid lava were free to move up or down in the conduit. Due to its greater fluidity, the pond generally rose or sank more rapidly than the plug. Crags of crusted lava projected through the lava lake much like islands in a lake, and at times the lateral shifting of these crags gave the false appearance of islands floating on the lake.

In Halemaʻumaʻu, lava rose through source wells and drained from the lake through sinkholes.

Eruptive activity within a crater often has little effect on the surrounding landscape (lower left). However, debris thrown out by high fountains, such as cinders from the 1959 Kīlauea Iki eruption, may permanently change nearby areas (left). The interaction between lava flows and ocean water provides the material that forms the island's black sand beaches (below).

A constant current flowed from source to sink. Crusts formed continually in the cooling surface of the lake, and cooling plates of crust often tilted on edge and sank into the fluid lava. Other fragments were swept into the sinkholes. Lava fountains up to 30 feet high rose above the surface of the lake. Some of them remained stationary above the underlying source wells or sinkholes.

At times the lava lake drained away completely, exposing the glowing lava that formed the bottom of the lake. At other times lake level sank, sometimes as much as several hundred feet in a single day. Each rapid sinking was generally accompanied by avalanches of glowing material from the walls of the crater, the floor of which was commonly obscured by dense clouds of dust-laden sulfurous fumes.

Explosive Eruption of 1924.

The lava lake in Halema'uma'u began to subside early in 1924, and was empty by February 21, leaving a pit 380 feet deep. On April 29, following an intrusion in east Puna, the crater floor began to collapse. Numerous earthquakes accompanied the subsidence, and instruments at the observatory indicated magma movement into the east rift zone. By May, the crater was 700 feet deep, with nearly constant rock falls from the unstable walls. On May 11 Halema'uma'u exploded, throwing rock fragments onto the floor of the caldera. Explosions continued during the following week, increasing in violence until, on May 18, great clouds of dust rose more than 20,000 feet into the air and blocks of rock, some weighing several tons, were blasted out of the crater. Violent lightning storms accompanied rains of mud. The walls of Halema'uma'u gradually collapsed, increasing its diameter from 1,400 to 3,400 feet. Following the May 18 blast, explosions decreased in intensity and ended on May 27.

Debris thrown out by the explosions contained a little new volcanic material but consisted mostly of fragments of the old solid walls of the crater. This indicated that the explosions did not originate within the magma reservoir but rather within zones of water-saturated rock above the reservoir. The great withdrawal of magma from beneath Halema'uma'u allowed ground water from surrounding rocks to flow into the conduit. The water flashed to steam as it encountered the hot walls of the conduit.

Under pressure from overlying rock debris, the steam escaped violently in a series of explosions, carrying with it rock fragments and dust. When volcanic heating of ground water occurs, such phreatic explosions can be anticipated.

Activity from 1924 to 1966. The steam explosions of 1924 marked the end of the continuous lava lake activity in Halema'uma'u, which had collapsed to a final depth of 1,300 feet. Over the next ten years, lava briefly returned to Halema'uma'u seven times, filling the crater to a depth of 760 feet.

Kīlauea was quiet for the next 18 years. It was 1952 before lava returned to Halema'uma'u, in an outbreak lasting four months. Then, following a shortlived eruption in 1954, activity became focused on the east rift zone. On February 28, 1955, the first erup-

tion to occur in the eastern Puna district in 115 years broke out along a 10-mile-long fissure system. For nearly four months fountaining lava threatened the village of Kapoho and entered the ocean at three locations along the Puna coastline.

Four years of quiet followed. Late in 1959, lava resurfaced, this time at the summit of Kīlauea in Kīlauea Iki crater. At first a line of lava fountains 1,200 feet long played along a crack on the southwest wall of the crater 300 feet above the floor. Cascades of lava poured into the crater, burying the old floor of 1868 lava. Eventually, activity became limited to one vent, which repeatedly sent fountains more than 1,000 feet high. At its peak, one fountain reached a height of 1,900 feet, the greatest yet recorded in Hawai'i. Cinder and spatter from the fountains piled up on the crater rim, building a conical hill

A lava lake in Halema'uma'u was very active through the early part of the 20th century with lava continuously visible in the caldera (left). The unusual explosive eruption 1924 (right) marked the end of that type of activity and the beginning of a quiet phase, which lasted until 1952. Lava appeared at the summit again in 1954 (above).

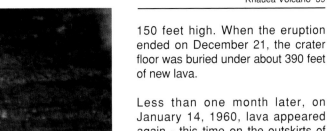

150 feet high. When the eruption ended on December 21, the crater floor was buried under about 390 feet of new lava.

Less than one month later, on January 14, 1960, lava appeared again - this time on the outskirts of Kapoho village, 28 miles east of the summit caldera. A few hours after the eruption began, activity was concentrated at one vent, where a voluminous double fountain reached heights of 1,500 feet. Lava poured eastward into the ocean and spread out to form a fan-shaped flow that covered an area of four square miles and destroyed most of Kapoho. During the 36-day eruption, the flow of lava into the sea created 500 acres of new land along the coastline. As magma fed the Kapoho eruption, the summit of Kīlauea subsided. Molten lava beneath the crusted floor of Halemaʻumaʻu that was left over from the 1952 eruption drained away. The floor of the crater collapsed, and a basin with three circular pits was formed.

Halemaʻumaʻu was the site of three brief eruptions in early 1961, and in September a middle east rift zone eruption extruded about three million cubic yards of lava. During this two-day event the deflation of the summit indicated that approximately 70 million cubic yards of magma had drained away, apparently remaining underground to form dikes in the fissures of the rift zone.

Kīlauea next erupted in early December 1962 with a minor outpouring in the upper east rift in ʻĀloʻi Crater (later buried by lava during the Mauna Ulu eruption, 1969-74), creating a small lake on the floor of the crater. During this eruption, it was estimated that more than 10 million cubic yards of magma were intruded into the rift, but only 430,000 cubic yards of lava reached the surface.

November 1959 Kīlauea
eruption began with a line
ountains along the wall of
crater. Activity was later
fined to a single vent (left).
a covered the floor of the
er and a spectacular foun-
which shot skyward was
asured at 2,000 feet in
ght. Less than a month
r, a rift eruption approxi-
ely 25 miles to the south-
t destroyed the
ge of Kapoho (below).

Three more intrusions of magma into the upper east rift were detected in 1963, but only two minor eruptions occurred (in August at 'Alae Crater and in October at Nāpau Crater). A March 1965 eruption between Makaopuhi and Nāpau Craters poured lava into both craters, forming a lava lake in each. A small eruption associated with major disturbances in the Koa'e fault system, partly filled 'Ālo'i Crater in December 1965.

The lava lakes within Kīlauea Iki, 'Alae, and Makaopuhi craters provided an opportunity to study the cooling of basaltic lava. Holes were drilled into the cooling lake crusts, and the depth at which molten rock was reached, and its temperature, were recorded. The Kīlauea Iki lake was first drilled in July 1960. Its upper crust was 19.5 feet thick, and the temperature at the base of the crust was 1,064°C. A year later the crust was 35 feet thick, and by 1967, 100 feet thick. The last drilling of the lake was done in late 1988. At that time, drillers encountered a

zone of partially molten lava 240 feet below the surface. This zone was 60-90 feet thick and contained less than 20% molten lava by volume.

Activity from 1967 to 1975.

Lava returned to Halema'uma'u in November of 1967 with vigorous fountaining and lava lake activity that continued for eight months, ending in July 1968. In August, a fissure opened across the floor of Hi'iaka Crater, three miles from the summit, and lava formed another lake. Although this was a very brief outbreak, the summit of Kīlauea sank more than six inches. In October, a three-mile-long fissure system opened, extending from Kanenuiohamo into Nāpau Crater; this eruption continued for two weeks. Activity resumed between 'Alae and Nāpau Crater for five days in February 1969.

On May 24, 1969, lava fountained from an east-northeast-trending fissure between Pauahi and 'Alae Craters on the upper east rift zone. Activity soon became concentrated at the central part of the

cientists were able to study e cooling rate of the lauea Iki lava lake by illing into the crust (left), st in 1960 and several ore times during the next 8 years. In 1988, there was ill a zone of partially olten lava deep within the ke. Many craters display a yriad of flows of different jes (above), as the result both flows that originate ithin the crater and those at erupt outside the crater nd pour over the rim.

fissure and, with only a few interruptions, continued for over five years. The frequent overflows piled layer upon layer of new rock around the main vent and formed a broad 400-foot-high lava shield named Mauna Ulu (growing mountain). This eruption was characterized by 12 episodes of high fountaining (up to 1,770 feet high) and vigorous flows in 1969 and by a sustained lava lake and overflows thereafter.

More than 12 miles of the Chain of Craters Road were buried during the Mauna Ulu eruption, and lava flows that reached the sea added 200 acres to the island. As lava entered the ocean, divers observed the behavior of lava beneath the water, including the development of pillow lava (bul-

bous lava masses resembling on-land pāhoehoe toes, characteristic of submarine lava flows), which no one had previously witnessed.

During the course of this long eruption, three minor outbreaks occurred in the summit region, including an eruption on the upper southwest rift zone, the first along this zone since 1919. Then, on the morning of July 19, 1974, the lake in Mauna Ulu drained away, leaving a yawning, fume-choked crater. Instruments at the Hawaiian Volcano Observatory recorded strong tremor and earthquakes, indicating that another eruption was imminent. A few hours later, fissures opened on the southern rim of Kīlauea caldera and in and south of Keanakākoʻi Crater. Spectacular cascades of lava plunged down the caldera wall and joined fountains on the floor, forming a flow that moved northward to a point below the Volcano House Hotel. Activity continued until July 22. This summit eruption marked the end of over five years of activity at Mauna Ulu, at the time the longest eruption on the east rift zone of Kīlauea in written history.

Following the July 1974 activity, the summit of Kīlauea started re-inflating. By year's end, Kīlauea had experienced two more brief eruptions: one in Halemaʻumaʻu, the other on the southwest rift.

The 1975 Earthquake. Tremendous stresses had built up inside the volcano, when, in the predawn hours of November 29, 1975, two powerful earthquakes rocked the island. The strongest shock measured 7.2 on the Richter scale and originated beneath the ocean floor, 18 miles southeast of the Kīlauea caldera. Downward movements along the many coastal pali accompanied a rapid sinking of the coastline from Kalapana – where the renowned black sand beach at Kaimū sank 2.5 feet – westward into the national park. At Halapē campground, the coastline subsided about 14 feet, submerging a

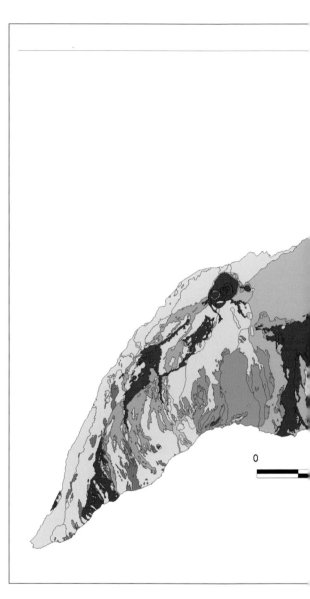

0

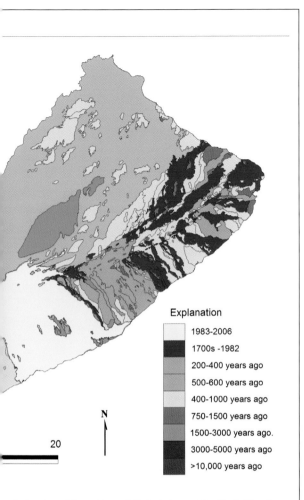

Explanation

■	1983-2006
■	1700s -1982
■	200-400 years ago
■	500-600 years ago
■	400-1000 years ago
■	750-1500 years ago
■	1500-3000 years ago.
■	3000-5000 years ago
■	>10,000 years ago

N

20

Geology from Wolfe and Morris, 1996, Geologic map of the Island of Hawaii

Kīlauea ("spewing, much spreading" in Hawaiian) lives up to its reputation as one of the world's most active volcanoes. Ninety percent of the surface lava flows on Kīlauea are less than 1,100 years old (above). Sulfur deposits (far left), lava-covered highways (left), and newborn cones (above right) are visual reminders of ongoing activity.

coconut grove. Two campers were drowned in the ensuing tsunami. The effects of the locally generated tsunami were felt as far as California, where waves damaged a few small boats. The earthquakes also triggered an eight-hour eruption in the summit caldera.

Activity from 1976 to 1982.

The 1975 earthquake apparently slowed the rate of summit inflation at Kīlauea, but three intrusions of magma into the middle east rift zone in 1976 and early 1977 indicated the possible renewal of eruptive activity. On September 11, 1977, volcanic tremor (caused by the movement of magma underground) accompanied a seismic swarm in the middle east rift zone. Two days later, lava broke out in the Puna forest reserve, 15 miles east of the summit. A fissure erupted for three weeks before the activity finally localized at a single vent where a new cone, named Pu'u Kia'i, formed. A lava flow moved rapidly downslope toward Kalapana, forcing the evacuation of that coastal village. On October 1, the eruption stopped, but the flow crept forward for three more days, halting barely a quarter of a mile from the nearest home.

It was November of 1979 before Kīlauea had reinflated to its pre-1977-eruption level. At 8:30 A.M. on November 16, lava erupted in Pauahi Crater and from fissures extending to the northeast and southwest outside the crater. Although this eruption lasted less than one day, it was viewed by more than 25,000 visitors. Rangers barricaded the Chain of Craters Road, which had been reopened only five months earlier after being closed for ten years as a result of the Mauna Ulu eruption.

Kīlauea was quiet during 1980–81, although nine intrusions of magma took place into the southwest and east rift zones. Two brief summit eruptions occurred in April and September 1982. Both were from east-northeast-trending fissures approximately one half mile long and lasted less than a day.

Activity from 1983 to present. Shortly after midnight on January 2, 1983, Kīlauea's summit began to deflate rapidly. Earthquakes migrated down the east rift zone, and, on January 3, lava erupted along fissures that extended nearly five miles downrift from Nāpau Crater. After six months of fissure activity (eruptive episodes 1-3), the eruption localized at the Pu'u 'Ō'ō vent, which straddles the eastern boundary of Hawai'i Volcanoes National Park. For the next three years (episodes 4-47), Pu'u 'Ō'ō erupted approximately every three to four weeks, usually for less than 24 hours. These eruptive episodes were characterized by spectacular lava fountains that catapulted lava higher than 1,500 feet above the vent. Fallout from the towering lava fountains built a cinder and spatter cone 835 feet high and fed channeled 'a'ā flows.

The flows posed an immediate threat to the sparsely populated Royal Gardens subdivision, located on a steep slope 3.5 miles southeast of the vent. 'A'ā flows reached the subdivision in as little as 13 hours during several eruptive episodes and destroyed 16 houses in 1983 and 1984.

In July 1986, the vertical conduit to Pu'u 'Ō'ō ruptured, and the eruption shifted to a new vent, Kupaianaha, 1.5 miles northeast of Pu'u 'Ō'ō. This marked the end of episodic high fountaining and the beginning of five and a half years of nearly continuous, quiet effusion (episode 48). A lava pond formed over the new vent, and its frequent overflows built a broad, low shield that reached its maximum height of 180 feet in less than a year. After weeks of continuous eruption, the main channel exiting from the pond gradually developed a roof as crust at the sides of the channel extended across the lava stream. Soon the lava stream was enclosed in a tube of its own making. Lava tubes insulate rivers of lava from both heat and gas loss, allowing lava to remain fluid and travel farther without cooling.

Late in November 1986, flows from Kupaianaha reached the ocean, cutting a swath through Kapa'ahu and closing the coastal highway. A few weeks later, the lava took a more easterly course and overran 14 homes on the northwest edge of Kalapana. From mid-1987 through 1989, most of the lava that erupted from Kupaianaha flowed directly to the sea. Steam explosions at the ocean entry fragmented the lava, creating black sand that collected to form new beaches in protected coves down-current of the lava entry. The largest beach formed at

An earthquake measuring 7.2 on the Richter scale shook the Big Island on November 29, 1975. Areas along the southern coast sank as much as 14 feet, submerging a coconut grove at Halapē campground (right). The inset photograph shows the same area before the quake.

Kamoamoa, where a small bay caught the sand; this beach was later buried by lava. New, but unstable, acreage was added to the island as lava deltas built seaward over a steep submarine slope of fragmented lava.

In the spring of 1989, lava flows overran the Waha'ula Visitor Center in Hawai'i Volcanoes National Park. The flows surrounded Waha'ula Heiau but did not cover it. A year later, the eruption entered its most destructive phase when flows turned toward Kalapana, an area cherished for its historic sites and black sand beaches. By the end of the summer, the entire community, including a church, store, and 103 homes, lay buried under 50-80 feet of lava. As the flows advanced eastward, they took to the sea, replacing the palm-lined Kaimū Bay with a plain of lava that extends 1,700 feet beyond the original shoreline. In late 1990, a new lava tube diverted lava away from Kalapana and back into the national park, where flows once again entered the ocean.

The eruptive episodes that began in January 1983 produ spectacular lava fountains (above). Over the next three years, the fountains built the foot-high Pu'u 'Ō'ō cone (fac page, top). Since 1987, colla over the Pu'u 'Ō'ō vent has formed a crater 1,300 feet in diameter (facing page, cente

In 1986, the eruption shifted Kupaianaha, where a lava po formed over the vent (left, wi Pu'u 'Ō'ō in the background). Kupaianaha was active until early 1992, when the eruptio returned to Pu'u 'Ō'ō.

Since 1992, vents on the sou and west flanks of Pu'u 'Ō'ō have fed flows to the sea. Spatter cones and rising gas plumes mark the location of these vents (facing page, bottom).

During the five and a half years that Kupaianaha reigned, repeated collapses of the Pu'u 'Ō'ō conduit gradually formed a crater about 1,000 feet in diameter. A lava pond was present sporadically at the bottom of the crater starting in 1987. The volume of lava erupted from Kupaianaha steadily declined through 1991. Concurrently the level and activity of the Pu'u 'Ō'ō lava pond rose. In November 1991, fissures opened between Pu'u 'Ō'ō and Kupaianaha and erupted for three weeks. Kupaianaha continued to erupt during this event, but its output was waning. On February 7, 1992, the Kupaianaha vent was dead.

Ten days later, the eruption returned to Pu'u 'Ō'ō. Lava erupted in low fountains along a fissure on the west flank of the massive cone. This was the first in a series of flank vents that would be active for the next 14 years. As at Kupaianaha, the style of the eruption was nearly continuous, quiet effusion. Flows from the flank vents quickly built a lava shield that banked up against the south and west slopes of Pu'u 'Ō'ō.

In November 1992, lava crossed the Chain of Craters Road in Hawai'i Volcanoes National Park and entered the ocean at Kamoamoa, seven miles from the vents. Over the next month, tube-fed pāhoehoe flows at Kamoamoa buried archeological sites, the national park's campground and picnic area, and a black sand beach formed earlier in the eruption. From the end of 1992 through January 1997, tubes fed lava to the ocean almost continuously, broadening the Kamoamoa flow field, which lies mostly within the national park.

Beginning in 1993, collapse pits appeared on the west flank of Pu'u 'Ō'ō as the magma feeding the flank vents undermined the

side of the cone. The largest of these, known as the "Great Pit," had engulfed most of the west flank by the end of 1996. On the night of January 30, 1997, magma drained from the Pu'u 'Ō'ō conduit, causing first the crater floor, and then the west wall of the cone, to collapse. Shortly thereafter, new fissures broke open and erupted briefly in and near Nāpau Crater. This event, designated episode 54, was over in 24 hours.

The collapse at Pu'u 'Ō'ō left a large gap on the west side of the cone. The rubble-lined crater was 700 feet deep, and for the next 23 days, no active lava was visible at the eruption site. Episode 55 began on February 24, 1997, when a lava pond returned to the Pu'u 'Ō'ō crater. A month later, new vents opened on the west and southwest flanks of the cone.

Tube-fed flows from the episode 55 flank vents added to the pre-existing Kamoamoa flow field, and lava reached the ocean in July 1997 near the eastern boundary of

Lava flows from the Kupaianaha vent claimed the Waha'ula Visitor Cent[er?] several park residences, a many adjacent archeologi[cal] sites in 1989. The steel beams of the building remained as a stark remin[der] (top) for several years; ev[en]tually these, too, were bur[ied] by lava. In 1990, flows tur[ned] toward the village of Kalapana (bottom), destro[y]ing over 100 houses. Waha'ula Heiau, built in approximately AD 1275 w[as] finally buried by lava flows August 11, 1997.

Hawai'i Volcanoes National Park. Flows continued to enter the ocean in this area for much of the next five years.

In May 2002, a new flank vent on the west side of Pu'u 'Ō'ō erupted on Mother's Day and was the main source of lava flows through 2003. New vents opened on the southwest side of Pu'u 'Ō'ō, in early 2004, first on Martin Luther King, Jr.'s birthday, and in March on the birthday of Prince Kūhiō Kalaniana'ole. These vents gradually stole the show, and by the end of 2004, the Kūhiō vent fed the only active lava tube.

Flows from this vent entered the ocean at various locations inside the national park from November 2004 until mid-2007. In June, the eruption pattern changed again, beginning with a brief fissure eruption uprift of Pu'u 'Ō'ō. In July, a new fissure opened between Pu'u 'Ō'ō and Kupaianaha, and by autumn, flows from the ongoing fissure eruption extended about four miles northeastward.

The Pu'u 'Ō'ō-Kupaianaha eruption is the first one outside Kīlauea's summit caldera in the last 500 years lasting longer than half a decade. By January 2007, almost three quarters of a cubic mile of lava had covered about 45 square miles and added almost 500 acres to Kīlauea's southern shore. In the process, lava flows destroyed 189 structures and resurfaced nearly 9 miles of highway with as much as 115 feet of lava. As of November 2007, the eruption gives no sign of winding down.

For the latest eruption information, visit http://hvo.wr.usgs.gov/

Since 1987 much of the lava from the Pu'u 'Ō'ō -Kupaianaha eruption has traveled to the coast via tubes and poured into the ocean.

Lava entering the sea creates huge steam plumes. Constant small explosions create bits of lava that collect in bays to form black sand beaches.

Haleakalā: House of the Sun

Erosion, not volcanic activity, carved the 3,000-foot-deep summit depression of Haleakalā on the island of Maui (below and right). Cinder cones and lava flows visible within the "crater" were produced by later eruptions. Haleakalā is considered dormant but not extinct. Each morning hundreds of early risers drive to the summit hoping to witness a spectacular sunrise.

HALEAKALĀ NATIONAL PARK
Haleakalā (house of the sun) is a large volcanic mountain, reaching 10,023 feet above sea level, which forms the eastern part of the island of Maui. It began as a typical shield volcano like Kīlauea and Mauna Loa. Thousands of thin flows of olivine basalt and closely related lava followed each other in rapid succession, until the shield had been built to an elevation of 7,000 feet above the present sea level. At that stage, the frequency of eruptions declined. Weathering produced soil layers on the surface of some flows before succeeding flows buried them.

Slow changes in the magma body beneath the volcano produced new rock types. The new group, known as the Kula Volcanics, consists largely of alkali-rich basalt, with some picrite-basalt rich in big crystals of olivine and augite. The alkali basalt was more viscous than pre-Kula lava and formed thicker, more massive flows that are well exposed in the walls of Haleakalā Crater. Picrite basalt containing large black crystals of augite forms the surface in the vicinity of the Haleakalā Visitor Center.

Volcanic activity decreased greatly by about 180,000 years ago. Erosional downcutting was able to outpace volcanic growth as streams carved their canyons into the mountain slopes. Large landslides on the south flank

allowed several small canyons to coalesce, opening a huge notch now known as Kaupō Gap. On the volcano's north flank, Koʻolau Stream cut back far into the heart of the mountain. These two major canyons joined to form Haleakalā Crater, a central erosional trough seven miles long, one and a half miles wide, and 2,000 feet deep.

Throughout this time, eruptions persisted along the rift zones, sporadically pouring lava flows from newly-formed cinder cones. But growth of the crater, which was well developed by 120,000 years ago, increasingly protected much of East Maui from lava encroachment. Deep weathering, gullying, and soil formation modified the landscape in those areas sheltered from a new lava blanket. Sharp contrasts developed where young lava flows abutted markedly older lava. Across East Maui, these younger lava flows, though similar to older lava of the Kula Volcanics, are commonly starker in appearance by virtue of their youth. They have come to be known as the Hāna Volcanics. Most of Haleakalā Crater today is covered by Hāna lava flows and cinder cones younger than 5,000 years.

Though its volcanic vigor has lessened, Haleakalā has continued to erupt every 200 to 500 years. It is the only volcano in the Hawaiian group besides those on the island of Hawaiʻi to show any recent activity. Its youngest lava, once thought as young as A.D. 1790, erupted sometime between 1449 and 1633, as measured by radiocarbon ages from two sites. The lava issued from

Kaupō Gap, on the southern side of Haleakalā (above), marks the headwall of a huge ancient landslide. The gap was partially filled by Hāna lava flows. A trail through the crater and gap provides the most direct route from West Maui to Hāna. Molokini Island, off the coast of Maui, is the top of an ash cone on the southwest rift zone of Haleakalā (left).

Kalua o Lapa cinder cone on the southwest rift zone, at an altitude of 575 feet, and flowed into the sea. This flow is crossed by the road that follows the coastline from Mākena to Keoneʻōʻio, at the head of La Pérouse Bay.

The Hawaiian Volcano Observatory

The U.S. Geological Survey's Hawaiian Volcano Observatory is perched on the rim of the Kīlauea summit caldera at Uwēkahuna. Next door, the National Park Service operates the Thomas A. Jaggar Museum, named in honor of the geologist who founded the observatory. Jaggar, a professor at the Massachusetts Institute of Technology, established the observatory in 1912 and remained director for the next 28 years.

Initially, the observatory was funded by the Hawai'i Volcano Research Association, a group of Hawai'i businessmen, and by MIT's Whitney Fund for research

The Hawaiian Volcano Observatory sits on the rim of Kīlauea caldera (above). The original observatory (left) was located near the present-day Volcano House Hotel.

Scientists at the observatory keep their fingers on the pulse of the active volcanoes with the aid of seismometers, GPS receivers, tilt-meters, and other instruments whose signals are continuously transmitted to the observatory.

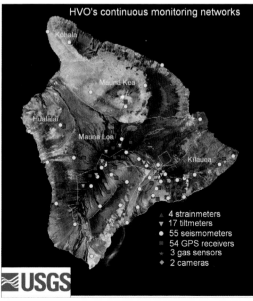

HVO's continuous monitoring networks

Kohala

Mauna Kea

Hualālai

Mauna Loa

Kīlauea

▲ 4 strainmeters
▼ 17 tiltmeters
● 55 seismometers
■ 54 GPS receivers
★ 3 gas sensors
◆ 2 cameras

≋USGS

in geophysics. In 1919, adminis-
tration of the observatory was
taken over by the U.S. Weather
Bureau, which at that time was
responsible for earthquake
investigations in the United
States. Between 1924 and 1948,
the observatory passed first to
the U.S. Geological Survey, then
to the National Park Service,
and, finally, back to the
Geological Survey.

The Hawaiian Volcano
Observatory was originally located where the Volcano House
Hotel now stands. When the present hotel was built in 1941, the
observatory moved, first to the
building that now houses the
Kīlauea Visitor Center, and, in
1948, to a building that was constructed in 1927 on the rim of the
caldera, near its high point at
Uwēkahuna. The 1927 building
now houses the Thomas A.
Jaggar Museum, and HVO occu-
pies newer quarters.

Scientists in the field collect
samples of fresh lava to ana-
lyze (top) and use a geoelec-
trical instrument to determine
the volume of lava flowing
through a lava tube (left). By
employing a global positioning
system (GPS) receiver to
measure the exact position of
a benchmark (right), geologists detect the swelling or
subsidence of the volcano due
to movement of magma
beneath the surface.

Since 1912, Kīlauea and Mauna Loa volcanoes have been under close scrutiny by the staff of HVO. The observatory continuously monitors volcanic and seismic activity by mapping active lava flows and tubes, sampling lava and volcanic gases, and analyzing the continuous stream of seismic, ground deformation, and other geophysical data that is transmitted automatically to the observatory or collected in the field. The data gained by monitoring are put to immediate practical use in forecasting eruptions, assessing hazards posed by ongoing activity, and issuing warnings. Longer-term research conducted at HVO is aimed at better understanding how volcanoes work and will result in better eruption forecasting and hazard assessment in the future.

Selected Bibliography

Decker, R. and B. Decker, 2007, Volcano Watching, 6th ed. Hawai'i Natural History Association, 84 p.

Decker, R.W., T.L. Wright, and P.H. Stauffer, 1987, ed., Volcanism in Hawai'i, 2 vols. U.S. Geological Survey Professional Paper 1350, 2506 p.

Hazlett, R.W., 2002, Geological field guide, Kīlauea Volcano, Hawai'i. Hawai'i Natural History Association, 121 p.

Hazlett, R.W. and D.W. Hyndman, 1996, Roadside Geology of Hawai'i. Mountain Press, 307 p.

Heliker, C., 1990, Volcanic and Seismic Hazards on the Island of Hawai'i. U.S. Geological Survey general interest publication, 48 p. Revised 1997.

Heliker, C., P.H. Stauffer, and J.W. Hendley, 1997, Living on active volcanos - the island of Hawai'i. U.S. Geological Survey Fact Sheet 074 97, 2 p.

Heliker, C., D.A. Swanson, and T. J. Takahashi, eds., 2003, The Pu'u 'Ō'ō - Kūpaianaha eruption of Kīlauea Volcano, Hawai'i: The first twenty years: USGS Professional Paper 1676, 206 p.

Heliker, C., and S.R. Brantley, 2004, The ongoing Pu'u 'Ō'ō - Kūpaianaha eruption of Kīlauea Volcano, Hawai'i: U.S. Geological Survey Fact Sheet 2004-3085, 2 p.

Macdonald, G.A., A.T. Abbot, and F. L. Peterson, 1983, Volcanoes in the Sea: The geology of Hawai'i, 2nd ed. University of Hawai'i Press, 517 p.

Sutton, J., T. Elias, J.W. Hendley II, and P.H. Stauffer, 1997, Volcanic Air Pollution—a hazard in Hawai'i. U.S. Geological Survey Fact Sheet 169-97, 2 p.

Wright, T.L., T.J. Takahashi, and J.D. Griggs, 1992, Hawai'i Volcano Watch: A pictorial history, 1779-1991. University of Hawai'i Press, 162 p.

CREDITS

PHOTOGRAPHS:

Bishop Museum: pg. 39 (lower), pg. 56 (lower).

English, T. T.: pg. 11 (upper).

Kjargaard, J.: pg. 55.

Lewis, G. Brad: pg. 36 (upper).

Peebles, D.: pg. 4, pg. 54.

Sharkbait Productions Hawai'i: pg. 6 (lower).

U. S. Geological Survey. N. G. Banks: pg. 43. S. Brantley: pgs. 52, 53. T. Duggan: pg. 29 (right). J. P. Eaton: pgs. 15 (upper), 39 (upper), 40, 45 (upper right). T. T. English: pg. 23 (right). J. Forbes: pg. 44 (lower). J. D. Griggs: cover, inside front cover, pgs. 13 (lower), 15 (lower), 22 (lower), 26 (lower left), 27 (lower), 28 (center), 31 (lower), 33 (top), 44 (center), 48 (upper), 49 (upper), 50 (upper), 51 (upper, lower), 56-57 (upper), 62. C. Heliker: pgs. 16 (lower), 17, 48 (lower), 49 (middle, lower), 58 (lower), 58-59 (upper, lower). R. T. Holcomb: pgs. 42, 47. T. A. Jaggar: pg. 38 (lower). P. W. Lipman: pgs. 4 (upper inset), 47 (inset). D. N. Little: pgs. 14 (center), 31 (upper). J. P. Lockwood: pg. 18. D. W. Peterson: pgs. 2, 27 (upper), 32 (lower), 61. D. Richter: pg. 41. D. Swanson: pg. 18 (inset). T. J. Takahashi: pgs. 24 (upper), 37 (upper), back cover. R. I. Tilling: pg. 4 (lower inset). D. Weisel: pg. 50 (lower). E. W. Wolfe: pg. 21.

U. S. National Park Service. Photographer unknown: pgs. 5 (upper), 17 (inset), 20 (upper and lower), 36 (lower), inside back cover. J. Erickson: pg. 27 (right). W. Fink: pg. 25 (lower). J. Jacobi: pg. 28 (lower left). L. Katahira: pg. 25 (right). G. Kaye: pg. 33 (lower).

MAPS AND ILLUSTRATIONS:

WORLD OCEAN FLOOR PANORAMA, pg. 7, by Bruce C. Heezen and Marie Tharp. © 1977 by Marie Tharp.

TECTONIC PLATES, pg. 8, modified from Tilling, U. S. Geological Survey.

HOT SPOT, pg. 9, by Paul Martin.

HAWAIIAN ISLANDS AND SEAFLOOR, pg. 11, from Eakins, et al., 2003, U.S. Geological Survey.

LANDSAT 7 MOSAIC, pg. 12, courtesy of the Hawaii Synergy Project, University of Hawaii.

OBLIQUE LANDSAT IMAGE, pg. 23, processed by U. S. Geological Survey.

MAP OF KĪLAUEA, pg. 35, U. S. Geological Survey, Hawaiian Volcano Observatory.

STRATIGRAPHIC MAP OF KĪLAUEA, pg. 44-45, from Wolfe and Morris, 1996, U. S. Geological Survey.

ISLAND OF HAWAI'I MONITORING NETWORK, pg. 57, U. S. Geological Survey, Hawaiian Volcano Observatory.

OTHER CONTRIBUTIONS:

Exterior cover design: Jamison Design/Jamison Spittler. Authors of previous editions: 1993, Tari N. Mattox and Thomas L. Wright, U. S. Geological Survey. 1989, Jon W. Erickson, U. S. National Park Service.

Volcanic Vocabulary

'A'ā – lava with a rough clinkery surface.

Andesite – a lava richer in silicon and generally of lighter color than basalt.

Ash – fine-grained volcanic ejecta of sand or dust size.

Asthenosphere – the part of the upper earth's mantle that can flow under pressure and which weakly transmits seismic waves.

Augite – variety of pyroxene commonly found in basaltic rocks.

Basalt – a dark, heavy lava rich in iron and magnesium, and comparatively poor in silicon; the common lava of Hawai'i.

Blocks – volcanic ejecta larger than 1.5 inches across, solid when thrown out.

Caldera – a large circular or oval volcanic depression.

Cinder cone – a conical hill built by fine ejecta around a volcanic vent.

Crater – a bowl-shaped depression, smaller than a caldera.

Dike – a sheetlike body of magma that cuts through older rock. A dike that reaches the earth's surface becomes the supply line for an eruption.

Ejecta – fragments thrown out by volcanic explosion.

Eruption – the forceful ejection of volcanic material onto the earth's surface.

Fault – a fracture in the earth's crust along which one side has moved with respect to the other, parallel to the fracture.

Fault scarp – a cliff formed by movement along a fault.

Fault zone – an area characterized by numerous parallel faults.

Fumarole – a vent from which volcanic gases issue.

Graben – a valley or trough bounded on both sides by normal faults.

Harmonic tremor – the continuous vibration of the ground caused by magma movement, generally detectable only by seismic instruments.

Hot spot – a stationary hot zone in the earth's mantle that partially melts the region just below the overriding crustal plate, creating pockets of magma. The buoyant magma rises through weak zones in the overlying rock and erupts to form volcanoes.

Intrusion – the injection of magma into pre-existing rock; also, the body of magma so formed. Many intrusive bodies never reach the earth's surface to erupt, but rather cool and solidify within the earth.

Kīpuka – an "island" of old land surrounded by younger lava flows.

Lava – hot liquid rock extruded onto the earth's surface, and the rocks solidified from it.

Magma – hot liquid rock beneath the earth's surface.

Microradian – an angle of ground tilt equal to about 0.00006 degree. A one-microradian increase in tilt would be equivalent to steepening the slope of a one-mile-long board by placing a nickel under one end.

Olivine – a green mineral composed largely of silicon, iron, and magnesium oxides.

Pāhoehoe – lava with a smooth or ropy surface.